WITHDRAWN

MEDIEVAL LIVES

Peasant

ROBERT HULL

A⁺
Smart Apple Media

Smart Apple Media is published by Black Rabbit Books
P.O. Box 3263, Mankato, Minnesota 56002

Printed in the United States

Published by arrangement with the Watts Publishing Group Ltd, London.

Library of Congress Cataloging-in-Publication Data

Hull, Robert, 1935–
    Peasant / Robert Hull.
    p. cm.—(Smart Apple Media. Medieval lives)
    Summary:"Traces the life of a typical peasant in medieval times from birth to death, including childhood,
marriage, work, holidays, and customs. Includes primary source quotes"—Provided by publisher.
    Includes index.
    ISBN 978-1-59920-172-6
    1. Peasantry—Europe—History—Juvenile literature. 2. Civilization, Medieval—Juvenile
literature. I. Title.
HD1523.H85 2009
305.5'6330940902—dc22

                                                                                2007046032

Artwork: Gillian Clements
Editor: Sarah Ridley
Editor-in-chief: John Miles
Designer: Simon Borrough
Art director: Jonathan Hair
Picture research: Diana Morris

Picture credits:
Arquivo Nacional da Torre do Tombo Lisbon/Alfredo Dali Orti/The Art Archive: 21. British Library, London, Courtesy of the Board
of Trustees: 26. British Library, London/The Art Archive: front cover, 11t, 20, 24, 29t, 33t, 33b, 36. British Library, London/Bridgeman
Art Library: 14, 41. British Library, London/HIP/Topfoto: 27. Biblioteca Nazionale Marciana, Venice/Gianni Dagli Orti/The Art
Archive: 35. Bibliothèque Nationale, Paris/AKG Images : 24. Bibliothèque Nationale, Paris/Bridgeman Art Library: 23t. Bodleian
Library, Oxford/The Art Archive : 23b, 30. Chris Howes/Wild Places/Alamy: 13. Lambeth Palace Library, London: Bridgeman Art
Library: 10. Musée des Beaux Arts, Ghent/Topfoto: 19t. Musée Condé, Chantilly/Giraudon/Bridgeman Art Library: 16, 18, 38, 40.
Museo Civico Bologna/Gianni Dagli Orti/The Art Archive: 34. Museo Civico Città di Castello/Gianni Dagli Orti/The Art Archive:
39. The Museum of London: 15t. Picturepoint/Topham: 5, 8. Private Collection, Switzerland/AKG Images: 37t. Roy Rainford/Robert
Harding Picture Library: 17. Ann Ronan PL/HIP/Topfoto: 31. Victoria and Albert Museum, London/Graham Brandon/
The Art Archive: 28.

9 8 7 6 5 4 3 2 1

CONTENTS

INTRODUCTION

The medieval period of European history is from approximately 1000 to 1500. It was a time of momentous events. In 1066, England was conquered by the Norman French duke, William, and his men. William was crowned king in December 1066. During most of the fourteenth century, France and England fought a series of wars called the Hundred Years War. In addition, Christian crusaders fought Muslim Arab armies over the control of Jerusalem. The Black Death, or plague, in 1348, killed about one-third of the population of Europe, altering the balance of society.

A peasant sows seeds. The medieval economy was based on agriculture.

Feudal Society

At the beginning of this period, European society was feudal. Kings owned all the land, but barons were granted land in return for service in war. Nobles made similar arrangements with knights, and they, in turn, with those below them, down to the peasants, who were granted a few acres of land in return for fees and work obligations. This network of agreements held society together.

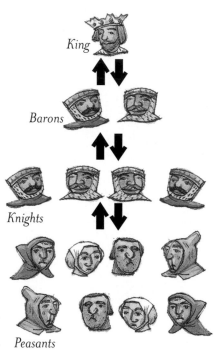

King

Barons

Knights

Peasants

Throughout the medieval period, great projects such as monasteries and abbeys, castles, churches, and cathedrals were built. Towns and trade flourished and grew, yet farming remained as important as ever. Most people worked on land that they did not own. In return, farmers owed work and fees (money, animals, or goods) to the lord or lady of the manor.

The Peasant Farmer

In many parts of Europe, the peasant farmer worked alongside others on strips of land scattered across two or three huge fields surrounding a village. In some areas, fields were arranged differently, and farmhouses stood on their own or in small hamlets. The peasant was "tied" to this land. He had to stay in one place if he wanted to carry on cultivating his few acres. If he ran away, as some peasants did, he would have no land to farm. He would be punished too, if he were caught.

In many ways, his life was not his own; he was a serf, neither a free man nor an outright slave. Unlike a slave, he had important rights that were part of the custom of the village. He had the right to take timber for houses from woodland and the right to speak in the village assembly, the "hall-moote."

The Peasant

This is the story of a typical peasant who worked 20 to 30 acres (8 to 12 ha) of land and lived in a village of 50 houses. We use the term peasant, but that word did not come into the English language until the fifteenth century. This peasant was "servile"—a serf or "husbondman" (a man bound to the land) with a house.

The peasant was seldom well-off and often miserably poor. He ate well when harvests were good, but famine struck often. Any of his children might die young or his wife in childbirth. In times of need, he relied on his neighbors. Otherwise, the peasant lived his life in a long struggle with the land, the demands of his lord, violence, and the ever-present risk of disease, illness, and death. Yet he often managed to enjoy life—he made the best of it.

Serf or Slave?

Nothing belonged to the serf. Even his children counted as the lord's possessions. This is shown by an eleventh-century French document that shares out serfs and their children:

❖ *We, the monks of Marmoutier and Gautier Renaud, held in common men and women serfs, who were to be divided between us…. Therefore, in the year of Our Lord 1087…in the time of Abbot Bernard, we proceeded to the division of the male and female children of several families.* ❖

Those names are listed and the document closes with:

❖ *There was excepted from the division one very young girl-child, who remained in her cradle. If she lives, she is to be our common property until an agreement is made to assign her to one or the other lordship.* ❖

FIRST YEARS

T**he peasant baby is born at home in the parents' bed. At the birth, the mother is helped by female neighbors and a midwife. Regardless of class, any birth is very risky. For every child who survives, there are usually baby sisters and brothers who do not. If things go wrong in childbirth, as they sometimes do, there is little that can be done. The mother dies, or the child, or both. But this mother is well and a baby boy arrives safely.**

Baby Days

The baby is carefully washed and wrapped in swaddling clothes, long strips of cloth bound around the body. This is constricting, but it is supposed to help his limbs grow straight.

After a few days when his mother is strong enough, she is "churched" at a service of purification in the village church. The baby boy is baptized at the font and is now a member of the Catholic Church. He is given the first name of one of the three godparents selected to help with his upbringing. According to the church, had he died without being baptized, his soul would have gone to hell.

The baby feeds on breast milk until he is about 18 months old. His first solid food is chewed for him in his mother's mouth and then fed to him on her finger.

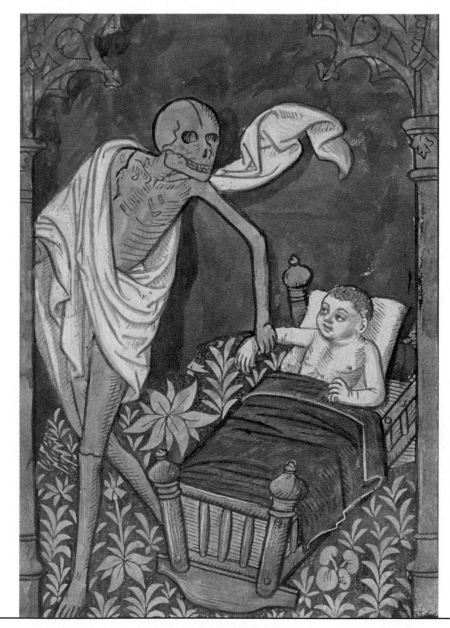

Death takes a child in this manuscript illustration.

Toddling

Soon he is toddling about and needs to be watched every minute. When he starts to walk, he has a walking frame to help him and prevent a fall or a hurried dash leading to one. He might go too near the fire in the hearth or the cooking pot. Animals are everywhere. A wandering pig out of its pen has a nasty bite. The boy gets dirty roaming about the house and outside in the lanes.

As he grows older, the little boy joins his older brothers and sisters in a shared bed. He is sung to and told stories and little rhymes.

There is much to watch in the first years. Inside the house, he watches his mother cooking over the hearth, brewing ale, and spinning wool. He watches his father carving wooden bowls, shaping stakes, or weaving basket fish traps.

Outside is just as interesting. Pigs dig with their snouts in the fenced yard, birds take seeds, visitors come down the lane, plows and carts roll by.

A peasant woman holds a baby indoors while a man chops wood outside in the snow.

PEASANT COTTAGE

The young peasant's home is a small house in a village. It consists of three bays or rooms: a bedroom, a hall or living area with a stone hearth, and a stall. It's smoky at times and can be cold and damp.

The house has a frame of curved timbers. These were cut from a suitable tree some distance away and brought to the village by the carpenters who did much of the work. They mounted the frame on stones, so the wood is above damp ground to prevent rot.

The church and village green with its pond were at the heart of most medieval villages.

Roof and Rooms

Materials for the roof and walls are easy to find. The roof is thatched with reeds and straw, and the walls are made from strips of thin wood (wattles) filled in with clay and animal dung.

The house is about 39 feet (12 m) long—longer than some houses in the village and smaller than others. It is about 16 feet (5 m) wide.

At the end of the hall space, on an earth floor, an open hearth with a fire is used for cooking. There is no chimney, so smoke from the fire drifts out of the door or the window openings. The windows have shutters and are covered with cloth in cold weather. Straw covers the floor.

Furnishings

The family has a locking chest for their best clothes, bed frames for the straw-filled mattresses, a table, a bench, stools, a washing tub, and a broom. They bought mugs and plates made of pottery and wood and a coarse glass jug from town craftsmen. They have spoons made from horn and other handmade articles.

The home is fenced in on its own *messuage* (space). There is a *byre* (barn) for animals and a building to store implements. They have a cart—which the neighbors borrow and sometimes forget to bring back! They tend a half-acre (.2 ha) garden to grow herbs, vegetables, and fruit. A dung heap provides fertilizer for the garden. The plot is surrounded by hedges and a wall, so there's some privacy. The door of the house has a lock.

From about the thirteenth century onward, farmhouses might be constructed of stone in areas where stone was plentiful. This photo shows a modern reconstruction.

Smoke-Free Zone

In later medieval Germany, the invention of the heated stove meant that bigger peasant houses could be kept more or less smoke free. The heated living area is a theme in poems by Neidhart von Reuental:

❖ *Megenwart's stube is large enough. Let's have a dance there on Sunday! His daughter says spread the news and come. Engelmar's preparing for dancing round the table.* ❖

CHILDHOOD

Beginning about the age of three, the little peasant boy plays continually. He plays with stones he picks up; he throws sticks in the stream and builds dams. He and his young friends make pretend houses and boats; they have little bows and arrows. They play cherry pit, rolling cherry stones to drop into holes. They also play marbles.

They have their slang talk and rhymes, too, and their cheeky calling games. They have little carved animals and carts. Some are homemade, one or two bought from craftsmen at the market or from traveling peddlers or chapmen.

Play and Games

The little boy mostly plays with other children out in the lane or in the fields, often alongside his father as he works. The village has its dangers—millponds and streams, horses with iron-shod hooves, cattle with long horns, pigs with fierce bites, even wolves sometimes; but he and his friends are free to roam and wander, though not too far.

Spoiled Children

A thirteenth-century French sermon given by a priest suggests that peasant children were spoiled at first, then treated more harshly:

❖ *Peasants spoil their children and make them little red frocks, and then, when they are a little bit older, they put them to the plow.* ❖

Medieval boys enjoy a swim.

This carved toy knight would have been a child's prized possession.

When the children are older, they play running, throwing, and balancing games. "Buck hide" is similiar to hide-and-seek; the "buck" hides from the hunter. Some games are seasonal. Climbing for nuts and fruit in autumn is a fun game—not work.

During Lent, the child plays with a top. In early winter, after the pigs are killed, the pigs' bladders are used to make balls. A bladder is filled with beans or dried peas or inflated and wrapped in cloth to make a ball.

Education for All

In all ranks of society, there were parents who wanted their children educated. In *Aelfric's Colloquy*, a teaching aid for monks written in 1005, the teacher asks:

❖ *Who are you here before me?*
Us boys. ❖

The boys include the sons of plowmen, shepherds, fishermen, merchants, shoemakers, and bakers.

Growing Up

The peasant boy is growing up fast, but he is not at school. Sometimes, his father sends him to the parish priest to learn to spell out and read letters and to sing. His friend's father decides his son should go off to the neighboring monastery to be educated and study Latin in order to become a monk.

The young peasant also prepares for his father's world of work. He drives ducks to the pond, collects hens' eggs, and fetches water from the well. He goes with his father to the fields and uses a stick to help drive the oxen along in front of the plow. He has to be careful— helping with cattle and horses can lead to accidents. Then, when he is 12, his father arranges for him to work a few days each week on the church's home farm to earn a penny or two.

Medieval Facts

By the time children were about the age of 14, their place in the world was decided by law. The church believed that, until they were 14, children were too young to commit sinful acts. The laws said children could not marry until then or take communion, and they did not have to make confession to the priest.

THE CHURCH

The parish church is at the center of the village and village life. From baptism to wedding to funeral, the most solemn moments of everyone's lives are celebrated or commemorated at the church.

Despite the church's importance, and the role of the priest in the parish, the priest is barely literate. He only knows the mass by heart, not the meaning of its Latin words. He is not a well-off man. He has to work the church's land, the "glebe," and has been known to store corn and keep sheep in the church.

A Farmer and a Priest

The priest was often a part-time farmer. Sometimes farming and religion clashed. In 1302, the parishioners of Saint Mary's Church in Devon complained that their vicar:

❖ *...keeps all manner of his beasts in the churchyard, by which it is badly trampled and vilely fouled...The same vicar also has his malt prepared in the church and keeps his corn and other things therein...* ❖

Peasants work hard to help support the priest in this manuscript picture.

Gathering Tithes

A fourteenth-century book for priests written by John de Burgo has this suggestion to help priests gather tithes:

❖ *Let peasants be questioned in the confessional whether they have defrauded by withholding or diminishing their tithes; ... whether they have withheld their bounden service to their lords.* ❖

Church Upkeep

Much of the priest's living comes from crops and cattle and sometimes money that the village peasants pay in tithes or tenths. In this way, the young peasant's father helps pay for the upkeep of the church. In theory, he gives the priest a tenth of all he produces and earns every year. Cattle and crops are called great tithes; others, such as hens and eggs, are lesser tithes. When the peasant dies, the church can take from his family a kind of death tax or a mortuary. This is usually the second-best animal; the lord has the best.

On Sunday, the family's best clothes are taken out of the wooden chest for mass. The church's colorful wall paintings depict God, the Virgin Mary, and Jesus; heaven and hell; birth and marriage; good and evil; and sin, love, hate, and good conduct. The young boy cannot read but finds the paintings very solemn.

In the Church

Everyone in the family goes to church. The young and the very young talk and even scamper about while the adults pay attention. The priest conducts the service in the chancel where the altar is behind the wooden screen. The congregation prays or repeats his words on the other side of the screen in the nave.

The church bells ring not just for mass and other religious festivals, but to warn the villagers of emergencies and to summon them to hear news. It is truly the villagers' church. Sometimes it is used as a refuge, a courthouse, or to brew ale or store corn. It even is used as a prison.

The Churchyard

The churchyard is used for anything from burials to games and festivities or singing and dancing— something the church often says it objects to. There is a story that some peasants found dancing in the churchyard on Christmas Eve were changed into trees for a year, "rooted to the spot."

Tithe barns, such as this English example, stored the portion of the harvest owed to the church.

Reading in Church

An Italian visitor to England in 1500 noted an interesting English habit—taking books to church:

❖ *They all attend mass every day, those who can read taking the office of Our Lady with them, and with some companion reading it in the church, verse by verse, in the manner of churchmen.* ❖

MARRIAGE

By the time the young peasant is 20, he wants to marry. To do so, he needs his father's consent. That will only be given when his father is ready to hand over the property and buildings to the son and the son's wife or when the son can provide his parents with a cottage and garden. Either that, or the father needs to be sure that he and his wife can continue living in the family house.

A priest reads the marriage service for the wedding of a young couple in this manuscript illustration.

Negotiating a Marriage

The next step is for the father to find a partner for his son. He will consider the daughters of men of his own status. Once a prospective bride is found, a go-between will be sent to her family to talk about a possible marriage. If everyone agrees, the young people will spend some time together for the next month or two to see how they get along.

If all these stages go well, the young woman's father will bring her over to view her prospective husband's house and holdings. The fathers will work out the business side of the union, especially the dowry the young woman will bring from her family and the land the young peasant will have. The girl's father will also pay a fine to his lord to receive permission for his daughter to marry.

Brueghel's painting from the 1500s shows people serving food at a wedding banquet.

The Wedding

The wedding ceremony is held at the church door and inside the church. Outside, the peasant states his gift dower—the goods, property, or money he gives to the bride. He places gold or silver and a ring for her on a shield or book along with pennies for the poor. They exchange vows; the priest blesses the ring. The peasant places the ring on his bride's middle finger and says, "With this ring I thee wed." He gives her the gold or silver and adds, "And with this gold, I thee honor."

They enter the church and the priest celebrates a Nuptial (wedding) Mass. Toward the end of the service, he covers the couple symbolically with a "care-cloth."

Afterward, merrymaking, games, and dancing in the churchyard occur. A celebration begins, leading to the supper which the bride's father agreed to provide.

Troth-Plight

In the eyes of the church, the young peasant and his possible bride have to consent to what is happening. If they agree and make promises to each other, even in private, that private "troth-plight" is, for the church, a binding contract which its courts will enforce as a marriage.

There needs to be a public agreement, or betrothal, to marry with a troth-plight or handfasting. The priest announces the banns at church, informing villagers of the forthcoming marriage and asking anyone who believes there is any reason for them not to marry to speak up.

Husbands Rule

A twelfth-century Welsh law says that wives need the husband's permission to dispose of things or even lend them and, even then, only to neighbors within shouting distance:

❖ *The wife of a villein may not give away anything without her husband's permission except her head-dress; and she cannot lend anything except her sieve and griddle, and that only as far as her cry may be heard when her foot is on her threshold.* ❖

Medieval Facts

A baby might be born to a couple before the wedding. The baby was made legitimate in the eyes of the church and the world by being placed under the care-cloth during the last part of the Nuptial Mass.

LAND

The young peasant's father has agreed to pass his house and land—his tenement—to his son. The newly married peasant and his wife share the house with his father and mother. The house is part of a "messuage." It has a piece of land or "croft" attached to it. The new wife, helped by her mother-in-law, will grow vegetables and look after the fruit trees as well as the pigs and hens. She may decide to grow flax and hemp for rope and textiles. It is an important part of the family's farming.

Medieval Facts

The land was plowed from the center outward. The earth turned inward to the right. This tended to heap the earth in ridges with furrows between each ridge. This also helped with drainage. The pattern of ridges and furrows still exists in some places.

Commons and Open Fields

At the edge of the village, there is common grazing land. Anyone's cattle can be pastured on it in restricted numbers to prevent overgrazing. This is where the peasant and his wife keep most of their cattle (for milk, butter, and cheese) and their sheep (for wool). The village cattle herd and shepherd are there to look after the animals.

Most of the peasant's back-breaking labor takes place in the large, "open" fields. An open field is one in which every farmer in the village has his own strips of land to work. Widths and shapes vary but tend to be narrow. Many are a furlong—a "furrow long"—in length. Some are longer and reach from the village to its boundary.

The strip arrangement is fair to everyone. Every farmer has a share of the best and the worst land. The farmers share equally in the chances of good or bad harvests.

Plowing with oxen, from an English manuscript, the Luttrell Psalter. *A psalter was a prayer book.*

guinem innocentem condempnabit.

Crop Rotation

The three village fields are rotated. A field may be sown with wheat one year and beans the next year. The third year it will be uncultivated, though cattle will graze and the manure will help the field recover its fertility.

The peasant needs oxen for plowing. He borrows the oxen and a plow. Most plows in the village are owned by groups of peasants or by wealthy peasants. He also relies on the help of other peasants for their labor. He will use most of the grain that he harvests from the 20 acres (8 ha) to feed his family. He will keep some as seed for the next year. About a quarter or a third of the grain will be sold.

The larger trees on the land will be useful for timber. He hopes to make money from selling wood for fuel. Some of the wood will be used for fencing. His wife keeps a few beehives under the trees and gathers the honey.

Young people dance to bagpipe music while sheep graze.

Medieval Facts

Not all peasants had rights of inheritance. In 1305, Scottish peasants petitioned Edward I (when he was occupying Scotland) for the same rights of inheritance as peasants in England.

WORK SERVICE FOR THE MANOR

The peasant does not own the land he now works. He is a tenant and not a free tenant, but a villein. He inherits this status, with the land, from his father. As a villein, he works on the land of lord of the manor throughout his life.

Workdays and "Boondays"

The workdays, fees, and rents that the peasant owes the lord are fixed by custom and recorded on the manor's court roll. The peasant works three days a week all year for the lord. The lord can also demand extra days of work, or boondays, in emergencies. Of course, these are the lord's emergencies. If it rains on some of the days when the peasants should be cutting hay for the lord, the lord may demand additional boondays from his tenants. They will lose time spent on their own haymaking. However, on boondays, the lord has to provide food and ale.

By hook or by crook—fallen or dead branches were used as fuel and helped to keep peasants warm.

Medieval Facts

The peasant had rights according to custom. They often had the right to pick up fallen wood for fires or to take any dead or dangling branches they could knock down from trees. Hence the expression, "by hook or by crook."

The fines and services owed to the lord vary greatly. This means that the reeve, the official appointed from among the peasants to look after the lord's interests and ensure the fines and dues are paid, is very busy and not popular.

The peasant also pays collective village taxes—taxes every villein pays. For instance, a "recognition" fine is demanded when a new lord inherits his estate. "Tallage" is a tax for little else than occupying the land. His poorer neighbors often pay their dues in pots and pans, beehives, or whatever they can.

In this manuscript painting for the capital letter "E," peasants pay the tax collector.

Not surprisingly, because work on the lord's land means losing time to work on his own land, the peasant works less hard and efficiently for the lord than he does for himself. Some lords find it cheaper to hire workers, especially as feeding the peasants on boondays can outstrip profits. Sometimes lords are willing to exchange the peasant's workdays for a cash payment from them; this suits some peasants.

Fees and Fines

Not only are workdays resented, but so are the fees or fines the lord takes. The peasant paid a fine to take over his father's land. When the peasant dies, his wife will pay "heriot," a death duty of the "best beast." For every right the peasant or his wife has, there seems to be a corresponding fine, expressed in terms such as "pork-due" or a "chicken-fine."

Servants bake loaves in a bread oven.

THE MANORIAL COURT

The young peasant has been to the lord's court with his father at various times since he was 12. Now he has to "pay suit" whenever the court meets, which varies from once every three weeks to three times a year. Someone acting for him will need to present the court with a good reason if he is absent—otherwise he will pay a fine.

Court Records

The court regulates and records details of the life of the village: its disputes, details of labor services, the fines and dues that peasants owe, and failures to pay the fines. Offenses such as trespassing, theft, and any violence of a minor kind (attacks on manor officials, brawls, and fights) are all dealt with in the court.

The peasant is told in advance when the court will meet. The lord of the manor or one of his top officials—the cellarer or the steward—makes the judgments. Other officials are present: hayward, ale-tasters, "tithing men," reeve, and bailiff.

All the peasant's agreements and transactions, those of his father before him, and anything to do with land, property, work, wages, and his legal status are recorded on the court rolls. It includes all fines, fees, and details of inheritance. If the peasant wants to know what land is assigned to him, he can find out from the court roll, with the help of someone who can read, usually the clerk of the court.

Although this picture does not depict peasants, it shows men paying dues to their lord.

A medieval court—in this case a royal court—with an offender being hanged (on the right).

The Court's Work

The peasant is familiar with the work of the court. In court, his father legally hands over the family tenancy to him. First, he relinquishes the land, and it reverts to the lord. Then the young peasant has to ask permission to take on his father's land. According to custom, tenancies are inherited, but the lord's right to it must be acknowledged. The peasant pays his entry fine to the court, in effect to the lord, and the tenancy is his.

One man wants his daughter to work outside the village. Another asks permission to send his son to school in the town. The lord is, in theory, losing the possible future services of a tenant so a fine is due. One peasant has put too many animals on the common grazing land. Another, who has allowed his house to become dilapidated, has had a stake driven in the ground in front of it to indicate the lord wants it repaired. Others have failed to report for haymaking on the lord's land and have spoken impudently to the hayward.

Much of it is routine, but occasionally dramatic stories appear: the death by drowning of a small child or the killing of a peasant. In all cases involving deaths, accidental or not, a royal coroner must be present.

Medieval Facts

The right to build a gallows and hang people belonged to the monarch; but some lords, nonetheless, did so themselves. The Abbot of Crowland was convicted of hanging a man who stole 16 eggs—though not on the abbot's land. The abbot claimed the right not only of "ingangenethef," the right to hang a thief caught on his own land, but of "outfangenethef," the right to hang a man he caught beyond the bounds of his manor.

Midwinter, especially the Christmas period, is a fine time of year for the peasant. He can take it easy for a few days and sometimes sit by the fire drinking or play with his children. One year's work is done, the next not yet begun. There will always be hens to feed and fences to mend, but the backbreaking seasonal work has not started.

Endless Work

Once this brief respite is over, the year is a round of nonstop working activities determined by routine and custom. The only interruptions to it are the lord's unpredictable boonday work demands, the equally unpredictable weather, feasts, festivals, and, of course, illness.

The peasant has to plow, cultivate, and sow his land in the open field. He will harvest the wheat, barley, oats, rye, peas, and beans. He also has to look after animals and shear the sheep.

This page from a medieval calendar shows peasants in a winter scene.

Singing Plowmen

A thirteenth-century book tells plowmen to be cheerful:

❖ *Plowmen ought not to be gloomy or irritable, but sing and be cheerful, and encourage the oxen in front of them with their songs. They need to take the cattle their straw and their feed, and to be fond of them, and stay with them in the stable at night. They need to make a fuss of them... When the plowing is finished it is the duty of the plowman and the husbandman to look after ditches, to dig, and fence, and repair all the watercourses in the fields, and do various other small useful jobs.* ❖

Spring and Summer

By February, the peasant's hard year is underway. In March, there is the pruning to do. In April, he plows, cultivates, and sows. When the plants start growing, there is weeding to do and birds to scare off.

July is the beginning of harvest. The peasant takes a sickle to the corn and gathers it in piles. He will use a pitchfork to load it onto an ox-drawn cart that will be hauled off to the barns. The corn will be threshed with flails—two lengths of wood joined by a chain—or he will let the oxen tread on it to separate the grain from the chaff. By Lammas (August 1), the cattle will be let out into the meadows to feed until spring.

Risking Fines

Later all the grain is, or should be, taken to the lord's mill to be milled into flour—at a cost to the peasant. Throughout the year, his wife takes bread dough to be baked in the lord's oven for another fee. Some bold families risk a court fine and use household querns to mill the flour, then bake their own bread—risking another fine.

Haymaking — from a medieval calendar — a June activity.

Autumn and Winter

At the end of summer, there are sheep to be sheared and fruit trees to be climbed to pick their fruit. The grapes will be trodden, and the wine making begins. In October, after the fallow land is plowed, the winter corn will be sown. The swineherd will take the pigs to the woods to feed. Acorns will be gathered to feed the pigs.

November, sometimes early December, is the "blood month." Many of the pigs, sheep, and oxen are killed and salted to preserve them for winter meat. There are still tools to be repaired, blades to be sharpened, fences to be mended, and ditches cleared.

But soon it will be Christmas again.

FEEDING THE FAMILY

The peasant family depends on the food it grows and that supply is always at risk. The peasant's father remembers a year when rodents destroyed most of a corn harvest and other years when rain flooded the fields and there were very poor harvests. He recalls epidemics of diseases among the cattle and sheep.

Peasant Produce

The family's food consists of vegetables and fruit from the croft garden, bread made from the corn harvest, and meat from animals killed at the start of winter. The farmer does the slaughtering, sometimes with a neighbor to help. Most parts of the animal will be eaten, even the intestines. Tripe, made from the cow's stomach, and brains are favorite parts.

Once in a while, they eat beef, mutton, or fatty pork—roasted or baked. People who live near the coast eat a lot of fish. Other meat might be from animals the peasant has poached—a rabbit or a game bird. But there are severe fines for infringing on the lord's hunting rights. A fish or two from the stream is easier and less risky.

Daily Fare

On most days, as well as bread, or instead of it, the family eats a kind of porridge or gruel made from oats and millet. Water or milk and

Peasants picking fruit.

salt are added to the grains of cereal, which is boiled for a few minutes. Flattened out into cakes, it can be fried to make a crude loaf of bread. The best bread, though, is made from more expensive rye or wheat and usually needs yeast or sour dough to make it rise.

The Garden Plot

In the plot by the house, the family grows vegetables, such as turnips and cabbage. They have apple and pear trees and grow raspberries, strawberries, and black

A peasant couple slaughter a pig while others make bread.

currants. The hens produce eggs; the cows and sheep provide milk, butter, and cheese.

Villagers drink water, whey, cider, and ale. The peasant doesn't trust the water and so drinks ale most often. He drinks mead occasionally, which is stronger and made from honey and water that is boiled and left to ferment. His wife collects

honey from her hives in the woods and also gathers wild herbs, dock, and sorrel.

They may eat quite well some years, but hunger and famine are part of the peasant's world. His father has told him about famine times and seeing things eaten— horses for one—that he doesn't want to think about.

SICKNESS AND HEALTH

When the peasant's diet is poor, all kinds of illnesses can occur. But even when food is plentiful, disease lies in wait, ready to strike, especially at the young. Funerals of babies and young children are a common sight in the village and not just in times of pestilence. There is always the danger of babies and mothers dying in childbirth.

Many medicines were based on plants, just like today. Manuscripts called "herbals" showed which plants could cure different diseases. Shown here are ivy (left) and a lime tree (right).

Pestilence

It seems that deadly diseases strike every few years. There have been years of the sweating sickness. Regularly in the winter, there are illnesses similar to it that have killed a number of people in the peasant's village.

Chest coughs are common. There is always the fear that someone in the family will get the type of consuming chest complaint that makes people sicken and die.

Other illnesses present threats. Sometimes lepers walk through the village with a bell to announce their approach. And there is madness. Not only demons, but the planets and moon are thought to cause it. It is also believed that people born under the influence of Saturn are gloomy and have skin complaints.

Medieval people believed that sickness was a punishment from God. In times of pestilence they took part in religious processions to try and appease what they saw as His anger.

Punishment for Sin

Most illnesses, though, or so the peasant believes, are God's punishment for sins. So he prays for good health for his family or for a cure when sickness strikes. He might even promise, some day when he has time, to go on a pilgrimage to a religious shrine.

For everyday troubles such as toothaches, colds, and aches, the peasant's wife picks herbs as remedies; village women say these always work. They are careful, though, to collect herbs at the time of day or night when the right planet is in the right place for the cure. And it is important to pray to God as well.

Expensive Doctors

Most peasants cannot afford doctors with their costly ointments, bloodletting, and cupping to draw blood. Town apothecaries are expensive with their compounds and medicines, such as the treacle. It comes from far away, takes 40 years to make, and is made of 100 ingredients including roasted vipers. That is the story the peasant hears.

People try charms, spells, and chants too, which they think work sometimes. People who are not doctors try bloodletting—sometimes with fatal results!

The Black Death

The Black Death of 1348 killed millions—a third of the population of Europe. A medieval doctor, Guy de Chauliac, wrote how the pneumonic, and then the bubonic, plague struck Avignon in France:

❖ *The plague began here in January and lasted seven months. There were two kinds. The first, with continuous fever and spitting of blood, lasted for two months; victims died within three days. The second, with continuous fever, and carbuncles and swellings, mainly in the armpits and the groin, lasted for the rest of the time, and victims died within five days.* ❖

WOMEN'S WORK

The peasant's wife makes bread and cooks for the family. She collects the firewood and makes the fire; she sweeps the house and makes the beds. Then there are the children to be fed and clothed and looked after. She keeps a close eye on the baby and toddler—indoors and out. She washes and mends all the clothes; the underclothes are washed regularly, the outer garments much less often.

Dressmaker

The peasant's wife makes most of the family's clothes. Some are made from the wool of their own sheep, which she has spun herself and then woven into rough cloth. Some are made from the flax they grow that she has turned into linen. Some clothes are made from lengths of cheap cloth she buys at the market or at the door from traveling peddlers.

The family's clothes are grey or black and must last a long time, so they often look shabby. The family does not wear anything colorful, except on feast days and holidays.

One or two rich peasants in the village dress as if they think they are merchants. They wear coats with bright buttons and decorated belts. They give their wives long dresses and silk hoods that are more suited to living in the town.

Beekeeping produced honey the peasant woman could sell.

Medieval Facts

Fashion for peasants changed in later medieval times. Men's loose tunics were replaced by short vests, buttoned waistcoats, and breeches became more like trousers. Women wore wider collars and more figure-fitting dresses that were pleated from the hips. The church expressed disapproval of changes that allowed more of the body to show.

This manuscript illustration shows women trapping rabbits. Whether they could do so legally would depend on what rights their lord claimed over wild game.

Farmworker

As if all the work around the house is not enough, she helps her husband out in the fields sometimes with plowing or haymaking. When her husband is in the fields, she sees to the pigs, the grazing sheep, and, of course, the hens and the ducks. She milks the cows and makes butter and cheese. She goes out by herself into the woods to collect fuel for the fire and herbs for cooking or medicine. She tends to her beehives and collects the honey. She has gleaning duties at harvest. She is responsible for walking to the manor house with the eggs, hens, ducks, butter, and all that is owed as dues at different times during the year.

The Plowman's Wife

This unforgettable picture of the peasant's wife and children at work with him in the fields comes from *Piers Plowman*, by William Langland, a fourteenth-century English poet:

❖ *His wife walked beside him with a long stick in a short coat with a winnowing sheet wrapped round her to keep off the cold. She went barefoot on the ice so the blood flowed. At the end of the row there was a small bowl, and in it lay a small child covered in rags, and two two-year olds were on the other side…and they all cried the same cry till it was sad to hear.* ❖

Weaving cloth on a loom.

EARNING MONEY

The peasant pays some of his fines and taxes to the lord or the king in cash. To do this, the peasant and his wife need to earn some money. Some of this extra income comes from selling the surplus vegetables and fruit from the cottage garden or some of the eggs or meat from livestock.

Extra Income

The family does not need to eat all the eggs from the hens and ducks, or all the raspberries and loganberries, or all the bacon from the pigs. The peasant's wife takes whatever they can spare and makes a few pennies selling what she can in the nearby town. The town is growing, and there is an increasing demand for fruit and vegetables, bacon and mutton, milk and cheese, and honey—exactly the things she can provide.

A visit to a town such as this one gave peasants a chance to sell surplus produce.

Medieval Facts

The ways in which village women earned cash for their families might include activities that the local manor court disapproved of. Emma Powel, a peasant woman of Ramsey, appears in the court rolls on charges relating to brewing ale, baking bread, working as a butcher, and selling "pudding"—probably homemade sausage. She was evidently successful in what she did; the charges stretch over a 50-year period.

When the children are older, she plans to add to her income by brewing and selling ale, as several other women in the village do, between other tasks. It will not be strong ale, but the peasant's everyday drink, which they have from early morning onward. She hopes to sell about 24 gallons (90 L) a week to make a bit of extra income.

Cash Jobs

There are opportunities for her husband to earn cash too, and not just receive payment in kind, meaning eggs, lambs, or wood, depending on what work he does and for whom. Since he now has oxen and a cart, he can work as a carter when his other work is done. Carting is always needed for moving dung, timber, stone, peat, animals, and foodstuffs.

Some of what he carts will be things he picks or gathers himself and takes to the town or the manor house to sell: rushes or sedge for thatching and wood for fuel or for the woodturner in the town. He can catch fish and do a small amount of hunting—especially birds. He takes his bow in the cart with him. His son is his helper.

Carting

This thirteenth-century letter to the Bishop of Chichester from his agent suggests how much work the carter might be needed for:

❖ *Can you send your long cart to Aldingbourne? So that on it I can send your venison up to London, with other food, and cloth for the poor, as much as you like, for I bought 300 yards at Winchester fair; I can't send your small carts because the time for sowing is near.* ❖

Carting was a valuable source of extra money.

GAMES AND ENTERTAINMENT

Peasant life is not all work. There are games that children and adults play together. There is music making and sport. Everyone looks forward to the next holy day or feast day, when work stops. In addition to attending church services, these festivals are times for celebration and entertainment with plays, dancing, minstrels, cudgels, pigbaiting and bearbaiting, tilting, wrestling, music, and drinking. These are a great release from the drudgery of working life but not an excuse to run wild.

Christmas

Christmas is the best time. No work can be done in the fields. The lord treats his tenants to a feast at the manor house. The peasant and his friends contribute by bringing the yule log and their own tablecloths, plates, and mugs. They also bring bundles of brushwood for the fire that will cook the meat. At the height of the fun, a man dressed as a hobby horse "gallops" in. He gives a horse-like neigh while tossing a painted wooden head and swinging a horsehair tail.

A few days later, there are the Twelfth Night fires with food and drink around 12 small fires in the fields or indoors—if it is raining—with candles.

Easter Season

During the Easter season, the peasant and his wife go to church frequently and give each other "pace eggs" which are decoratively painted hard-boiled eggs.

Fifteenth-century Christmas fun in the Great Hall of a noble house.

Nutcrack Night

What we call Halloween was the medieval Nutcrack Night. A couple who were about to be married put two walnuts or hazelnuts, one each, into the embers of a fire. The nuts either crackled and split, for the love to come, or burnt silently, for future indifference:

❖ *If he/she loves me, pop and fly.*
If he/she hates me, lie and die. ❖

Easter

Eleanor of Aquitaine (1122-1204) came to England in 1152 to be queen to Henry II. When a courtier listed for her the many customs of the 120-day Easter cycle, she impatiently interrupted him:

❖ *But what is particularly Easterly?*
His answer:
Morris dances, mystery plays, and pace egging. ❖

At a 1439 conference in Calais, France, to discuss terms at the end of the Hundred Years War between France and England, several participants failed to turn up because they had been injured playing football.

When local rivers froze, peasants could skate. Medieval winters were much colder than those of today.

Neighbors walk to the nearest town to visit the fair and to watch the mystery plays—religious dramas performed by the men and women of a particular trade group.

The subject of the mystery play matches the profession of the group of tradesmen, or guild, that is putting it on. The carpenters put on a play telling the story of Noah's Flood because it was members of that craft who built the ark.

On May 1, men and women go out into the woods to cut a branch and bring it back to the door of their house. The peasant helps to put up the maypole for the village to dance around. He looks forward to learning who will be queen of the May.

Sports and Games

During the year, there are plenty of sports and games—from rooster fighting and wrestling to quieter sports such as archery, dicing, board games, and fishing.

There are plenty of occasions and excuses for drinking strong ale. Each of the main events of the farming year calls for its own celebratory ale, such as the "scythe ale" when the corn is cut. Every village wedding had its "bride ale." There are also tithe ales, lamb ales, midsummer ales, Whitsun ales, and bid ales—all stronger than everyday ale.

Medieval games included football (right) and hoop rolling.

One game that may be played on these occasions is called "bringing home the bacon." Couples claiming they have not quarreled in the last year are questioned about their claim. The couple that cannot be trapped in a lie or inconsistency wins a side of bacon.

FREEDOM

In the worst times, the peasant has thought of trying to escape from his tied land, with its endless labor, services, and fines. He has heard that if you run away and live on the demesne lands of the king or in a chartered town for a year and a day, you are free—if you are not caught, brought back, and fined for running away. Other men have been lucky enough to marry free women; that in itself has freed them.

Buying Freedom

Gaining freedom is easier for those with less land—cottars or land holders with only 4 or 5 acres (1 or 2 ha). They can gain their freedom by paying the lord a modest fine. Those with more land can too, but they have to pay more. Freedom might also be gained by undertaking an obligation, such as promising to return to the village court every so often or coming back to work at harvest. Those who wish to enter the church gain their freedom. One boy in the village went to the monastery to learn Latin and become a priest. The boy will become free, although his father had to pay the lord a fee granting permission for his son to enter the church. Only a few peasants want a religious life for their sons.

Having made his fortune, a free man returns to the manor to help with the harvest.

38

One reason for falling farm yields in the fourteenth century may have been a change in climate leading to rainy, wet summers. That and the plagues may have driven many peasants from their villages. The following inscription on the wall of Ashwell Church may have been carved by a villager as he left:

❖ *The first plague was in June 1300. [Lower down:]*

The plague or pestilence of 1349. [Then:]

1350: wretched, wild and driven to violence the people remaining become witness of a tempest. On Saint Maur's Day this year 1361 it thunders on the earth. ❖

Leaving for the Town

The peasant also knows he could escape to the town and look for paid work. He already earns some extra money from his carting and from his wife's sale of produce and her ale brewing. Between them, they might eventually earn enough to buy most of their food instead of producing it from their land.

Villagers come and go. Some villagers have left for good. One widow on her own, whose son had gone off to school in the town, paid the various fines, rents, and money payments instead of workdays and finally bought her freedom for 30 shillings.

Once there were 30 or more houses in the village; now there are only 20. There is less social life now with only two ale brewers. The peasant labors on.

A fourteenth-century Italian town. Many peasants from the country went to towns and earned enough to buy their freedom.

LAST DAYS

The peasant is old and ill. He is worn out with ceaseless labor. In his late forties, he has outlived several of his friends and survived outbreaks of disease in the village.

Inheritance and Fines

His land and possessions will pass to his children, but his widow is entitled to a third of everything while she lives. There will be the lord's claims on his inheritance—the heriot of the best beast and the fine on the tenement, as well as the church's right to take the second-best beast. He worries that the lord might demand a higher entry fine to the tenancy from his son or try to change the family's holding to a lease—one that lasts for only a set number of years.

Fear of Death

He fears death. The priest's sermons and the pictures in church taught him of pits of fire and brimstone. Fiends with blazing eyes wait to pitchfork their victims into the great flame of fire that is 10 times hotter than any fire in the earthly world.

Neighbors visit. In a small village, everyone is aware of an approaching death. No doctor comes, though. Only richer people in towns can afford doctors.

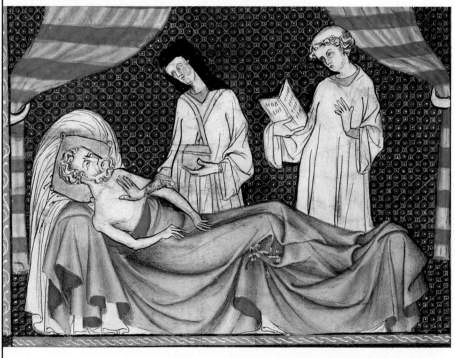

A parish priest anoints a dying man with holy oil as he gives him the last rites.

While the funeral takes place, a man digs the grave for the final resting place.

Medieval Facts

One estimate of the lifespan of medieval peasants, based on evidence in court records at Halesown in Worcestershire, suggests that once peasants survived to about 20 years old—which many did not—those who were better off, such as yardlanders, lived for another 30.2 years; those less well off, smallholders, lived for another 20.8 years.

He comes to administer the sacrament of Extreme Unction, the ceremony of the final anointing.

The peasant makes a final confession of his sins and is given the bread and wine of the eucharist.

The Priest

A small procession arrives at the home of the dying peasant, led by the priest who is followed by chaplains and clerks carrying a bell and a candle, holy water for sprinkling on the peasant, and oil for anointing him. With these, the priest brings the power to grant absolution for the peasant's sins.

Misbehavior

The wake was usually performed seriously, but there are reports of watchers becoming drunk and misbehaving. A court roll entry for the Abbey of Ramsey in 1301 describes how the watchers:

❖ *...in returning threw stones at the neighbors' door and behaved themselves badly, for which the neighbors raised the hue on them. Therefore the reeve and beadle are ordered to sue them in the court.* ❖

Wake and Burial

When the peasant's short life is over, he is laid in the best room in the house. A fire is lit, candles burn, neighbors gather around.

Then comes the wake. Family, neighbors, friends, and other farmers keep watch over the body through one long night. Cakes and ale are provided.

They are all at the funeral, a few carry the coffin from the church out into the yard. Most of the village crowds into the churchyard, where he is buried on the southern, sunny side.

GLOSSARY

Acre ❖ a measurement—five acres equals approximately two hectares

Apothecary ❖ someone who mixes up medicines

Banns ❖ the priest calls the banns three times in church, states a couple's intention to marry, and asks whether anyone has an objection to the marriage

Betrothal ❖ being engaged to marry

Bondman ❖ someone who is not free—a type of serf

Boondays ❖ extra workdays demanded by the lord of the manor

Cellarer ❖ a monastery official responsible for food supplies and trade with the world outside

Clerk ❖ a churchman, or a literate scholarly man, or someone looking after accounts

Commons ❖ grazing land and woodland within the village boundaries which could be used by all the villagers

Confession ❖ the private act of admitting sins to a priest

Cot ❖ a small house

Court roll ❖ the record of a court's decisions, called a roll because the parchment it was written on was rolled up

Cudgel ❖ a short stick used as a weapon and in sport

Demesne ❖ part of a manor farm directly farmed by its lord

Dowry ❖ a gift of money, land, or possessions that a woman brought with her into a marriage

Due ❖ an amount to be paid

Fair ❖ lords were granted fairs to allow the sale of goods of all kinds and entertainment in one place

Feudalism ❖ the system of holding land in return for agreed services or works

Fine ❖ a fee or charge

Free ❖ the condition of not being servile or bound to the land

Furlong ❖ the length of a furrow, about 220 yards (201 m)

Gleaning ❖ picking up ears of corn left on the ground by the reapers

Hamlet ❖ a settlement smaller than a village

Handfasting ❖ clasping of the hands in betrothal

Hayward (or heyward) ❖ a village official responsible for arranging the hay harvest

Heriot ❖ a due payable to the lord on the death of a tenant, usually the best beast, sometimes the finest piece of clothing

Lord ❖ the male tenant of a manor, usually a noble or knight; the lady of the manor is a female with the same rights

Manor ❖ an area of land ruled by a lord, with its own manor court

Mass ❖ the main religious service of the church, enacting the ceremonial consumption of bread and wine, the body and blood of Christ

Money ❖ pounds (£), shillings, and pennies, or pence, were the main coins used in Britain in medieval times. A mark was a coin worth 13 shillings, 4 pence.

Mortuary ❖ the due paid to the priest on a peasant's death, usually the second-best beast

Mystery play ❖ a biblical story acted out by members of a craft guild

Nobles ❖ high-ranking people such as lords and archbishops; also a coin

Payment in kind ❖ payment with articles of produce, such as eggs

Priest ❖ the clerk in charge of the church; sometimes a rector or vicar (meaning substitute for rector)

Plighting troth ❖ making a promise to marry

Pounds ❖ *see* money

Reeve ❖ a manor official elected from among villagers; his duties were to organize the peasants' work for the manor and ensure collection of their dues

Seize ❖ possess

Serf ❖ an unfree person tied or bound to land they hold from a lord; a bondsman or villein

Shepherd ❖ a peasant put in charge of village sheep

Shillings ❖ *see* money

Slave ❖ a person in the absolute ownership of another

Swineherd ❖ a peasant put in charge of village pigs

Tenement ❖ an area of land with a house attached, rented from a landlord

Threshing ❖ separating the grain from the stalks and husks by hitting the harvested corn with a flail—a long, hinged stick

Tithe ❖ the annual payment due to the church or lord of one-tenth of the serf's produce

Troth-plight ❖ loyalty or pledged faithfulness

Villein ❖ a peasant tied to the land who farmed strips of land

Wake ❖ the ceremony of watching, overnight, the dead person's body before burial

Yardland ❖ about 30 acres (12 ha); sometimes a "virgate"

Yardlander ❖ a holder of about 30 acres (12 ha) of land

Useful Medieval History Web Sites

www.fordham.edu/halsall/sbook.html
A Web site where you can read many original documents.

www.learner.org/interactives/middleages/
A user-friendly Web site on medieval town life, religion, homes, clothing, arts, and entertainment.

www.medieval-life.net/famines.htm
This Web site provides information on medieval history, life, family, and literature.

www.mnsu.edu/emuseum/history/middleages/contents.html
Enter this Web site and choose a guide (knight, merchant, nun, or peasant) or topic and learn more about medieval life.

Note to parents and teachers:
Every effort has been made by the publishers to ensure that the Web sites in this book are suitable for children, that they are of the highest educational value, and that they contain no inappropriate or offensive material. However, because of the nature of the Internet, it is impossible to guarantee that the contents of these sites will not be altered. We strongly advise that Internet access be supervised by a responsible adult.

TIME LINE

ca. 1000	Europe experiences a great expansion in its population over the next 200 years.
ca. 1000	A heavier wheeled plow, which cuts deeper, replaces the lighter "hook" plow across Europe; the use of horses in farming increases.
1066	William of Normandy invades England and is crowned king in December.
1096	The First Crusade begins.
ca. 1100	Over the next 200 years, there is a great expansion of peasant settlement in Europe.
ca. 1100	The three-field agricultural system is gradually introduced across much of northern Europe.
1135–1154	Civil war breaks out in England.
1146–1254	The Second through Seventh Crusades occur.
ca. 1190	The first windmills are built in Europe.
ca. 1200	Some peasant houses are being built of stone in northern Europe.
ca. 1200	In northern Europe, horses replace cattle to pull heavy loads.
ca. 1200	Money rents replace labor services across Europe. There is a growth in towns, trade, and the economy. There is an increase in the supply of coins and a demand for luxury goods.
1205	The River Thames freezes and can be crossed over the ice.
1207	The Order of St. Francis is formed in Italy.
1208	King John quarrels with the Pope, who bans church services in England.
1252	Henry III is given a polar bear, which swims in the River Thames with a muzzle and chain.
1260	The cathedral is consecrated in Chartres, France.
1265	Marco Polo travels to the Far East.
ca. 1270	The oldest paper manufacturing is Christian Europo in Fabriano, Italy.
1279	England introduces new silver coins.
1285	Spectacles are made in northern Italy.
ca. 1310	The mechanical clock is perfected.
1317	Europe experiences heavy rain and ruined harvests; famine spreads across Europe.
1323–1328	The peasants revolt in the Netherlands.
1337	The Hundred Years War between England and France begins.
1344	The English make their first gold coin.
1348–1349	The bubonic plague (Black Death) spreads through Europe.
1361	Europe experiences another outbreak of the plague.
1362	William Langland writes the poem *Piers Plowman*.
1369	Harvests fail across Europe.
1381	The Peasant's Revolt occurs in England.
1387	Chaucer begins writing *The Canterbury Tales*.
1388	The first town sanitation act is passed in the English parliament.
1437–1438	Many parts of Europe experience the plague, ruined harvests, and famine.
1438–1440	England experiences heavy rain and ruined harvests.
1430–1470	England experiences economic crises—many peasants are ruined.
1470	An economic revival begins.

43

INDEX

These are the lists of contents for each title in *Medieval Lives*: